v

REALLY WILD REPTILES

GECKOS

By Kathleen Connors

Please visit our website, www.garethstevens.com. For a free color catalog of all our high-quality books, call toll free 1-800-542-2595 or fax 1-877-542-2596.

Library of Congress Cataloging-in-Publication Data

Library of Congress Cataloging-in-Publication Data

Connors, Kathleen.
 Geckos / Kathleen Connors.
     p. cm. — (Really wild reptiles)
 Includes index.
 ISBN 978-1-4339-8365-8 (pbk.)
 ISBN 978-1-4339-8366-5 (6-pack)
 ISBN 978-1-4339-8364-1 (library binding)
 1. Geckos—Juvenile literature. I. Title.
 QL666.L245C66 2013
 597.95′2—dc23
                                        2012019130

First Edition

Published in 2013 by
Gareth Stevens Publishing
111 East 14th Street, Suite 349
New York, NY 10003

Copyright © 2013 Gareth Stevens Publishing

Designer: Ben Gardner
Editor: Kristen Rajczak

Photo credits: Cover, p. 1 © iStockphoto.com/Mark Kostich; pp. 5, 9, 19 Cathy Keifer/Shutterstock.com; p. 7 B&T Media Group Inc./Shutterstock.com; p. 11 (main) Meawpong3405/Shutterstock.com; pp. 11 (inset), 21 (tokay, leopard and giant geckos) Eric Isselée/Shutterstock.com; p. 13 Trahcus/Shutterstock.com; p. 15 Jim Merli/Visuals Unlimited/Getty Images; p. 17 Vibe Images/Shutterstock.com; p. 20 Bronwyn Photo/Shutterstock.com; p. 21 (web-footed gecko) dirkr/Shutterstock.com; p. 21 (banded gecko) fivesports/Shutterstock.com.

Printed in the United States of America

CPSIA compliance information: Batch #CW13GS: For further information contact Gareth Stevens, New York, New York at 1-800-542-2595.

Contents

Words in the glossary appear in **bold** type the first time they are used in the text.

MANY GECKOS

Have you ever seen a small lizard walking across the ceiling? It might have been a gecko!

Geckos are small **reptiles** with a big head and round eyes. There are almost 1,000 **species** of geckos. They range in size from about an inch (2.5 cm) to more than a foot (30.5 cm) long. Many geckos have green and brown skin. Some are colorful, such as the red-spotted tokay gecko. These lizards have some pretty wild features! Read on to learn more.

What a Wild Life!

Many gecko species have a long, thin tail. However, some, such as the knob-tailed gecko, have a short, flat tail or almost no tail at all!

A gecko's skin looks pebbly, but it's soft to touch.

5

IT'S ALL IN THE EYES

Scientists sort geckos into two groups. One group can move their eyelids to blink. The other group doesn't have eyelids at all! Instead, these geckos have a clear covering over their eyes to keep dirt out.

A gecko's eyes can tell a lot about its habits. Most geckos are nocturnal, which means they're most active at night. Their **pupils** are **vertical**, which helps them to see well in dim light. Diurnal geckos, or those active during the day, have round pupils. All geckos have sharp eyesight.

What a Wild Life!

Geckos without eyelids lick their eyes to keep them clean and wet.

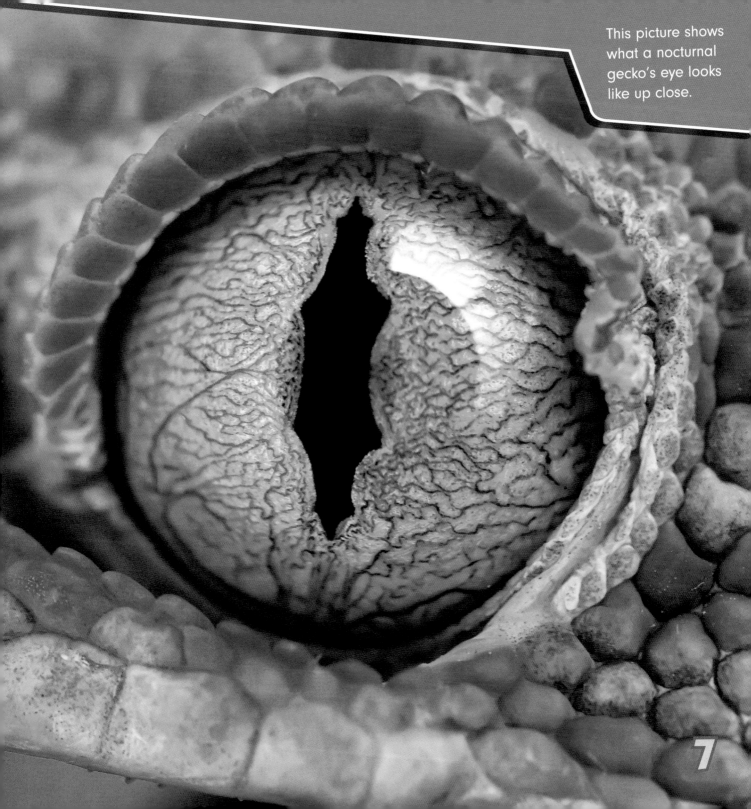

SUPER SENSES

A gecko's ears are small holes on both sides of its head. If you looked into a gecko's ear, you might be able to see straight through its head!

Geckos don't just use their nose to smell—they use their tongue, too! A gecko sticks its tongue out and picks up odor **particles**. The tongue carries them to Jacobson's organ, which is a small group of **cells** on the roof of the gecko's mouth. Then Jacobson's organ sends a message to the gecko's brain about what it smells!

What a Wild Life!

Geckos and many other lizards have a third "eye" on top of their head called the pineal (py-NEE-uhl) body. Scientists think it helps lizards tell the time of day.

If you see a gecko sticking its tongue out, it might be smelling something!

9

STICKY FEET

In some areas of the world, it's common to see small geckos in your house. These fast-moving lizards won't hurt you. However, they might be difficult to catch and get rid of—especially if they stand on the ceiling!

Millions of little hairs called setae (SEE-tee) grow on geckos' feet. Each of these hairs splits into even more tiny branches. The **friction** caused by the **angle** at which the setae meet the wall is what lets the gecko "stick" to it.

What a Wild Life!

A gecko can drop off its tail if a **predator** tries to catch it. The tail keeps moving as the gecko tries to get away. A few weeks or months later, a new tail grows!

11

TALKING GECKOS?

Geckos are the only reptiles that have a "voice" to make more than simple sounds. By clicking its tongue against the roof of its mouth, a gecko can make many sounds that mean different things. For example, a tokay gecko might hiss or croak at an attacking predator.

Geckos call to each other, too. They may use a barking sound to find a **mate** or claim their territory. From clicks to squeaks, the sounds a gecko makes depends on its species.

Common gecko predators include birds and snakes.

13

LET'S GET TOGETHER

Except for the 4 or 5 months of the mating season, geckos like to live alone. The male gecko will sound his mating call to let a female know it's safe to come closer. During the rest of the year, geckos guard their territory against any animal—including other geckos—that might eat up their food supply.

After mating, female geckos commonly lay two white eggs at a time. During mating season, female geckos may lay eggs as often as once a month or more.

What a Wild Life!

Some female geckos like to lay their eggs under leaves or bark, or bury them. Female tokay geckos stick their eggs to the sides of trees or rocks.

Female geckos of some species use their back feet to shape their eggs as the shells harden.

HATCHING

Like many reptiles, gecko mothers leave their eggs before the babies hatch. The size of baby geckos depends on its species. They often look like tiny copies of adult geckos. These little lizards don't have to look for food right after hatching. They shed their first layer of skin and eat it!

A gecko's life span varies greatly between species. Some geckos in the wild only live about 5 years. However, leopard geckos have lived as long as 30 years in **captivity**.

What a Wild Life!

Geckos found in New Zealand and New Caledonia give birth to live young.

Gecko hatchlings aren't very friendly. They bite!

17

GECKO HOMES

Geckos commonly live in warm places. These lizards have been found on every continent except Antarctica! Many geckos like to live in trees. The web-footed gecko, which has nearly see-through skin, lives in Africa's hot, dry Namib Desert.

Geckos eat mostly bugs, though they may eat fruit and plants, too. Some large species eat other lizards. If geckos live in your house, you've got built-in pest control! Geckos will eat roaches and other bugs that commonly bother people.

This leopard gecko found a cricket meal!

19

GECKO PETS

Many geckos live in the wild. However, they're popular pets, too. Tokay geckos and leopard geckos are some of the most common geckos kept as pets.

Do you want to own a gecko? These wild reptiles need a sturdy tank and lots of water. They're happiest when they're warm. It's important to know if you have male or female geckos if you have more than one. Don't keep two males together—they'll fight each other!

Awesome Geckos

tokay gecko

leopard gecko

giant Madagascar day gecko

web-footed gecko

banded knob-tailed gecko

21

GLOSSARY

angle: the space between two lines starting from the same point

captivity: the state of being caged

cell: the smallest basic part of a living thing

friction: the force that resists motion between two things that are touching

mate: one of two animals that come together to make babies. Also, to come together to make babies.

particle: a tiny bit of matter

predator: an animal that hunts other animals for food

pupil: the black part in the center of an eye that takes in light

reptile: an animal covered with scales or plates that breathes air, has a backbone, and lays eggs, such as a turtle, snake, lizard, or crocodile

species: a group of living things that are all of the same kind

vertical: straight up and down

FOR MORE INFORMATION

Books

Craats, Rennay. *Gecko*. New York, NY: Weigl Publishers, 2010.

Silverman, Buffy. *Can You Tell a Gecko from a Salamander?* Minneapolis, MN: Lerner Publications, 2012.

Websites

Geckos

kids.nationalgeographic.com/kids/animals/creaturefeature/geckos/
Read more about geckos, and see cool pictures and videos.

Reptiles

kids.sandiegozoo.org/animals/reptiles
See lots of pictures of different reptiles. Learn more about this amazing animal group.

Publisher's note to educators and parents: Our editors have carefully reviewed these websites to ensure that they are suitable for students. Many websites change frequently, however, and we cannot guarantee that a site's future contents will continue to meet our high standards of quality and educational value. Be advised that students should be closely supervised whenever they access the Internet.

INDEX